# Chief Cultural Officer

## 8 Pillars toward Sustained Global Influence

By Roberto Masiero

**First Edition:** May 2020

Chief Cultural Officer: 8 Pillars toward Sustained Global Influence/ Roberto Masiero

ISBN: 978-1-7351624-0-9

Publisher: Renaissance Evolution Inc.
601 Pennsylvania Ave. NW, South Building, Suite 900
Washington, District of Columbia, 20004

# A Message from the Author

Any great leader must be part visionary, master convener, and culture influencer. Visionary because you must predict where the future is trending and how individuals will respond. You do this through trend analysis, operational research, and well-informed intuition. Master convener because collaboration requires willing people but also someone to put the right people in a collaborative space and frame of mind. You achieve this through a combination of people skills and technological expertise. Culture influencer because more people means more variation and potential chaos. Creating organizational music that generates revenue is the goal. You accomplish this through a centralization of information that supports access, understanding, and trialability. As people arrive to solve problems, they bring their strengths to engage comfortably in the system of interaction—the culture intentionally created. With artificial intelligence and blockchain-based social interactions the Chief Cultural Officer is a necessary position leveraging both institutional knowledge and novel technologies.

Roberto Masiero

# Table of Contents

# Preface: Introducing the CCO

We typically have seen prosperity as a function of initiative and innovation. From stories of garage-based start-ups that became global giants to long-standing companies that reinvent themselves through new products and services, the potential seems limitless. However, the central question for many concerns the reach of this age of prosperity and the role of corporations and government to ensure equity, social good, and even justice. Recent global events have shown that the survival and resilience of nations depend upon its infrastructure born on the backs of essential workers. While corporations looked for support and the governments struggled with a balanced response, health professionals, grocery stores, food banks, and fast-food services managed the onslaught of families in need of the basic human needs.

The place for corporations and governments exists. The new experience must also include an active recognition of the value of the human element that spurs innovation. This focus must define, operationalize, and govern the learning, economic, and impact elements of the institutions wishing to innovate. A handful of corporations have implemented the basics of this attention to the human element in the form of a Chief People or Diversity Officer.

This document argues that institutions can go a step further and create more value with the Chief Cultural Officer (CCO). In addition to the person-centered sensitivity that values each of the workers at multiple levels, the CCO is tasked and skilled with managing the cultural nuances of the workers as well as the corporate culture inside and outside the corporation. The goal is to create a suitable bridge for the communication of context and value both from the corporation outward and from the host culture inward.

**C-Suite Position & Global Influence**

The Chief Cultural Officer is a C-Suite position that innovates the discussions of corporate processes, outcomes, and impact. The skillset of the individual chosen for this position is as critical as their position within the company or organization. C-Suite ensures access to the conversations that create culture across the enterprise. A focus on culture recognizes the latest is organizational and human behavior understanding that people operate best when the environment is constructed for the desired outcomes. Thus, the leadership of the CCO is both person-centered as well as systems focused.

Globalization is old news, but the potential for leveraging global access, international diversity, and complex markets remains a significant part of any successful company's strategy. Such leverage can suggest novel products and services or enable tremendously lucrative, unforeseen opportunities for any corporation.

**Pillars: Learning, Economic, and Impact**

The qualifications and context required for the CCO are presented as the first section of this text. Section 2 presents the eight pillars and their implementation with examples. It may be useful to consider the these in 3 groups: Learning, Economic, and Impact pillars.

- Learning pillars reference the ongoing training and corporate development in areas of competence/humility, wellbeing, and ethics.
- Economic pillars address the economic systems and markets including leveraging diversity, inclusion, and access for economic gain.
- Impact pillars refer to outcomes extending beyond the corporation to engage and improve life from others through the overlay of culture, language, and diversity.

**For Example: The CCO (Chief Cultural Officer) as an asset in Africa**

A friend from the Vatican Office of Communication, Janvier Yaméogo shared the following perspective:

> Good behaviors are those preserving harmony and peace in the community's web of relationships, harmony with nature (care of the environment), ancestors and God.

> For African ancestral wisdom, harmony, peace, unity, and dignity are essentially blended and based on the vital and collective consciousness to care for these sacred ties spiritually and materially according to time and space order.

> For ancient African wisdom, human being is an integral part of creation and not the peak of creation. Therefore, richness resides in the human ability to build and care fair and upright relationship. This is accurate development of harmonious relationships.

> Development is connected to the concept and reality of holistic harmony. Leadership means being at the service of this harmony. And most of the African tradition has a concept which promotes solidarity: Ubuntu (South Africa), Ujamaa (Tanzania).

> This means "We exist of one another", "I am because we are" and the CCO (Chief Cultural Officer) methodology suits perfectly to the Ubuntu philosophy, or better said Ubuntu behavior or Ubuntu leadership style.

Effectively Ubuntu means that our humanity is shared, that we value kindness, and we support one another because of the people we strive to be...

Globalization, as far as Africa is involved, is dominated by capitalism expansion with preference towards individual interest. However, Africans became converted to what Karl Polanyi named "fictitious commodities" and so the neoliberal form of globalization became for but not only Africans a deadly poison.

Ubuntu can help correcting the wrong direction of Globalization by reforming the global order or human behavior at the international level is to transpose the localized values of tolerance, human dignity, consensus, respect for others, compassion, and the pursuit of the common good to the activities of nations within the international system.

We can avow that if CCO (Chief Cultural Officer) sounds new as a human resources management technique, we can encourage research and find it in this indigenous African Ubuntu system as an old yet new way to underscore humanness, communalism, and participatory decision-making in global dealings.

Consequently, we are sure that the application of the CCO, a part of the Renaissance Evolution methodology, one already in action via practical applications already seen in African countries sets a standard of generating better people interaction in the future.

The capacity in African cultures to recognize the role of others in making us who we are and in expressing gratitude, reciprocity, dignity, harmony, compassion, and humanity in the interests of building and maintaining community, is known as Ubuntu.  Definition available at: https://en.oxforddictionaries.com/definition/ubuntu.    There    is certainly a component of Ubuntu in the Chief Cultural Officer methodology.

# Section I: A Network of Global Influence

# Chapter 1: The Epicenter of Opportunity

Simply stated, culture describes the exemplary actions, model behavior, and expected outcomes in carrying out the mission of for-profit organizations and donor intent of non-profits. Culture forms naturally from the interactions of people in the organization. But it can also be directed and structured according to best practices and a slew of sustainability considerations. Such considerations are a function of compliance managed by human resources and culture construction necessitating another, more encompassing senior management position. Enter the Chief Cultural Officer (CCO).

It is important right away to acknowledge and appreciate the role that Human Resources (HR), Diversity and Innovation divisions have played in supporting the needs of culture in the organization. A common saying in business states, "Culture eats strategy for lunch." No matter how great your strategy, the corporate culture determines how and how well employees implement and sustain strategy. HR and other divisions have traditionally incorporated a responsibility for culture in their compliance requirements. These lead training and education around cultural competence and ethics in the workplace, while perhaps also focusing on team building and synergy. Yet, the perspective is necessarily rooted in compliance. The point is to reduce the risk and exposure of the organization of employees that are untrained or ill-equipped for the diversity of the global workplace.

The innovation of lifting that responsibility from HR and other divisions is to also expand the footing of the cultural competence discussion in the organization. The motivation moves from compliance to learning, economics, and impact. The learning is like the HR doctrine but includes more intentional sharing and expression by employees. Economics relates to the intentional and coordinated ways that culture can be calculated for the bottom line of organizational balance sheets. Impact relates to the expansion of opportunity and influence while leveraged beyond the organizational experience in multiple ways.

Our learning objectives in this chapter are as follows:

- Allow employees to enter the organization as whole people including culture and expression of culture as a normal interactive opportunity and a value-add to the organization.
- Coordinate the activity, opportunities, behavior expectations, and outcome tracking that supports culture exchange, education, and experience.
- Facilitate the execution of the value proposition arising from holistic support of culture expression and the connection of people to impact.

**Expression**

Respecting the whole person is harder than it sounds. Throughout professional history, corporate cultures have been punctuated with secrecy and policies, spoken and unspoken, to leave a part of yourself at home and assimilate to the collective. This means that respecting the whole person is fist an unlearning process before becoming a learning process. Understandably, trust is a consideration here. Employees may be reluctant to be and reveal themselves fully in the corporate environment for fear of being shunned. Yet this blacklisting occurs by self-selection when employees, for example, do not smoke, attend happy hours, or participate in other social organizational activities.

Integrated people are characterized by both performance and vulnerability, perseverance and self-care, confidentiality, and communication. Vulnerability is never a comfortable proposition. The work environment is an especially important place to "never let them see you sweat." But vulnerability that is expressed within the team can produce positive outcomes overall. The team can meet the needs of team members proactively rather than waiting for something disruptive or catastrophic to occur in a production cycle. Self-care is critical to high-level functioning in the corporate space. This means knowing how and implementing a routine for anxiety, loss, and interpersonal management. It is as much about what is done outside of work as inside. Many corporations are recognizing the need for training and workspaces or work schedules that support self-care. Communication is perhaps the most misunderstood and misused element of corporate / organizational expression. Every message does not need to be initiated or curated by the boss. We can share salary information and religious practices. We can talk politics and religion in the office. We must learn and practice how to do each these with skill, respect, empathy, and intentionality.

Individual expression in corporate environments is vital to corporate goals including team building, collaboration, and employee retention. Team building must recognize that conformity is the enemy of grand ideas. Discussion to create compromise or new understanding from dissenting or other perspectives, is vital to innovation. When building teams, this means that people must shift from the idea of getting along with colleagues to facilitating fruitful discussions, disagreement and problem solving must be at the heart of these interactions. Effective collaboration requires honest communication. Honesty includes the expression of who you are as a person. To leave elements out, threatens to subvert the collaboration before it begins. Employees that are supported intentionally with environments that respect them holistically are more likely to remain with that company. This decreases the costs of marketing, brain drain, knowledge management and rehiring. It also retains the brain trust and the investment made in the development of the labor force.

### Coordination

This level of expression does not happen by accident. The history of what is perceived as appropriate corporate behavior is a difficult habit to break. Coordination will mean new methods of team support, cultural training that addresses humility, and cultural interaction that promotes the value of diversity of expression.

Team Support could for example include coordination of holiday observance and family day providing coverage for those who need to miss work. Holidays for multinational / diverse entities are varied and may be connected to religious practices or other form of meaningful events in different cultures. Family days can be sick days or requested vacations to care for family members either young, spousal, or elderly. Both holidays and family emergencies may be absorbed into company labor policies. The challenge is to maintain the functioning and cohesion of the team when these off-days occur. The team chemistry must be solid to result in the type of understanding required in these situations. Flexible schedules that include after-hour or weekend work may help. But the basic element of coordinating these efforts is information that is shared among all team members while focusing on the needs of individual employees. Always strive to seek agreement and understanding early to ensure high-functioning teams.

Cultural humility is still taking root in licensure and professional standard requirements. Many still refer to this construct as cultural competency. The difference is that humility describes active refusal of the assumption that you know about a person even if you have previously learned about that person as part of a group. This humility sets the requirement of dialogue among parties. It stimulates cultural exchange and understanding when coordinated well.

Diversity typically refers to areas like religion, gender, age, and more individual characteristics. But diversity of expression is also an important consideration. This means that emotions and meaning are communicated in different ways. Acceptance and appreciation of varying ways of communicating can solve many interpersonal conflicts before they start. For example, personal space may differ between two people. Another example, a person may use their hands or more physical demonstrations when they talk when compared to others. The meaning should not be obscured by a focus on the method of expression in communication.

### Facilitation

Facilitation describes the process of systematizing holistic expression of culture and a direct connection between people, their diversity/difference, and their impact within the organization. Multiple ways exist to affect the system-wide implementation of these ideals. Typically, training and performance review are included. Increasingly, hiring practices, team building, and extracurricular office functions include attention to diversity among cultures.

Holistic expression of culture, results in employees that are more whole. In such an environment, organization members bring more to the table than their labor, they bring their expertise along with their honest limitations. As teams work to complement each other, they build bonds and increase a collective productivity. Hiring practices should screen for employees that are open to this type of collaboration and mutual support. Team building should include a review of possible / likely cultural differences without outing individuals. Differences that will spark discussion, deeper thought, and creativity. Extracurricular functions should be augmented to be accessible to all employees regardless of whether they eat meat, drink alcohol, or are lactose intolerant. In short, cultural expression is accepted when the barriers to entry and enjoyment are lowered for all people involved... for humanity IS diversity of people, thoughts, and actions and as such it should be mirrored in corporate / organizational environments.

Impact however is often more difficult to track than outcomes. This leads some to believe that it is too difficult to achieve and not worth the effort. Yet, impact can be tied directly to outcomes and quantified in similar ways. For example, a common outcome from training is increased performance on a posttest or assessment after the training is completed. The impact of that outcome can be constructed as the intention of the training. The training may be intended for implementation by employees. If you count the number of times that the new learning is implemented, you have a tangible idea of the impact. You understand that the implementation instances increased due to the training. This is a solid impact. You can go a step farther and surmise that the implementation facilitates a certain cultural norm as was the initial intention.

# Chapter 2: The Art of Human Connectivity

The art of human connectivity is a culture negotiation proposition. People connect when they find a complement or a shared aspect of belief, norms, behavior, or goals. Typically, corporations / organizations script these and hire according to the existing cultural mandate through mission and vision themes. More recently, multinational corporations are recognizing that culture from one locale does not directly translate into new environments for several reasons. All the reasons boil down to culture and human connectivity. The opportunity is to move into markets with greater understanding and appreciation of the host culture. The cultural humility required is more than a general respect, it is translated into mechanisms of mutual benefit between the organization, employees, and the communities they reside in. This skill begins with the ability expressed within the organization itself. The organization must be competent and ever adaptable internally prior to generating effectiveness externally.

Our learning objectives in this chapter are as follows:

- Articulate the cultural capital evident within your organization.
- Create mechanisms for mutual benefit within the organization that model external mutually beneficial relationships.
- Identify the culture, language, and diversity needs that are needed in the form of new partnerships, new hires, and other relationships.

**Assessment**

Defining Cultural Capital. Before we begin, we need to define capital. Capital is anything that has value to an individual and may be traded among individuals creating an opportunity for exchange. This is the foundation of economics and the ideation of commerce. Capital has various forms. We often engage with financial capital - money. Many have trouble seeing or understanding other forms of capital. But there are three others in addition to financial capital. These include human capital, social capital, and cultural capital.

Human capital is composed of the abilities that reside within an individual that may be utilized to produce some output greater than the resources input. An example is education. A modest education can provide a means for exponential knowledge growth and untold breakthroughs in science and literature. Social capital is the capability that results from the collaboration between individuals or from the individual potential for collaboration. We often think of them as best exemplified through networks of people like in a social club or network marketing group. But the same principle is present in a family, church, or sibling group. i.e. Two heads are better than one.

Cultural capital is our focus. It builds on the shared norms, beliefs, and behaviors of groups to describe the creation of traditions or patterns of behavior that are not subject to the whims of any one person. The ability to influence this sense of what is normal, right, or true is the power of cultural capital. To understand cultural capital is to understand how policies and procedures are created, how orders are followed without question, and how organizations collectively persist.

Identifying Key Informants. The first step in any cultural assessment is to identify the information that will serve as the basis for the cultural exploration. Culture is one of those types of capital that relies heavily on the primary source of information decidedly dependent upon place and context. This necessitates the use of key informants. The beauty of cultural humility in persons, places, and context is that an individual is not a representative of its culture. They are an information source. Variations are expected to exist among different persons, different places, and in different contexts.

Identifying key informants begins with inviting people to share details about their cultures. It is a good exercise in refusing stereotypes or selection based on appearance. The key informant must accept the opportunity. It is commonly accepted today to question an individual's qualifications as a key informant. Questions of how diversity, difference, and culture become relevant in their worldview, are common to job applications. The point is often not to identify an academic knowledge base, but to assess the individual's interest to persist in the role and responsibility as a key informant.

Place is critical to understanding the information being provided by the key informant. It is a mistake to see the information as roadmap or rule book. Even when accepted as commonly accepted behavior, ensuring an understanding of place is important. This may be explained most simply through the differences in language as related to place / location. The language spoken at home is different than the language expected in the workplace. Key informants can keep you from speaking out of turn, utilizing words that are offensive simply based on the place in which they are spoken.

Context may seem like a consideration of place, but it has a significant difference. Whereas place is about the location where culture is expressed, context includes the people in their roles and how culture is expressed or viewed around them. Keeping with the spoken language example, we understand that place makes a difference in the experience. Yet the people who are present in the home would change the expression of language as well. For example, in many cultures, more respect and formality are practiced in multiple settings when an elder is present. In a church or synagogue, the practice may be more of reverence than careful language selection. These location / setting-based context considerations are vital to successful cultural navigation.

Organizing Sources of Knowledge / Optimizing Knowledge Management. Once the information is collected, it must be stored in a reliable, central location that is accessible by all stakeholders. Preferably, it would have varying levels of access and the ability to tailor presentations for specific populations. It is natural to think of this knowledge source as a computer system or some technological intervention, but other more human interventions are possible. Many organizations find it useful to supplement and support organic growth of their technologically supported cultural knowledge source with a team of cultural educators and guides.

The supplemental role of the "culture educators" is an extension of the CCO role and responsibilities. It is not overstepping to suggest that this team is the hands and fingers of the CCO. They are keenly aware of both the internal culture of the organization and the external best practices just as the CCO. These individuals are also involved in training functions, cross-functional teams, and other performance teams. They deliver information and are the first ears who listen to feedback.

The organic growth support role is one that extends from the team's engagement throughout the organization. As they bring the ethos back to the CCO, new training topics are assigned and developed. These training topics are encapsulated in the technological solution and the benefits and value of that intervention grow as the organization grows.

### Complementing

Mechanisms for Mutual Benefit. Humans are motivated by mutual benefit. More precisely one would say that humans are inspired by mutual benefit. Without covering the specifics of behavioral economics, suffice it to say that inspiration is more important than motivation. Creating mutual benefit is about structuring inspiration. You accomplish this sustainably through systems change more than through individual change. Structural or systems change means creating the environment for individuals to operate within rather than policing their behaviors.

Systems change requires modeling in addition to policy change. This includes relationship modeling as well as interaction modeling. The next step is cultural sharing within formal and informal groups. Formal groups are created through designation of organizers and coordinators. The Chief Cultural Officer would be instrumental in creating the hierarchy, reporting and informational structures, as well as outcome reports for the formal groups. Informal groups are the natural result of teams and social connections that occur within the workplace. These social connections are often due to natural affinity based on culture, demographics, or shared experiences. The CCO can support these by ensuring that social spaces and social time is a norm within the organization. Surveys and focus groups are useful to gauge the creation, impact, and opportunities created by informal groups.

The CCO must structure and communicate the mutual benefit. Typically, this proposition is a function of where people fall within the culture value spectrum. The basic values are in 4 categories: person, purpose, propinquity, and perspective. At their core, each is a choice between the primacy of the individual versus the collective. That distinction can be misleading though because it is a false dichotomy. Rather than an either-or distinction, it is more sustainable to consider each as a complementary cycle of choice behaviors centered in the motivation of everyone. The point of inspiration is to direct the choices toward the behaviors that intentionally support the desired outcomes of the organization.

*Modeling External Benefit Relationships.* The CCO must balance the goals of the organization with the sensitivities, circumstances, and proclivities of the community at large. This is not just a function of ensuring employee moral within the company. It is vital because the experiences of the employees within the organization are influenced by the cultural occurrences outside it. In short, employees bring their personal lives into work no matter what.

*The 4-P value categories* must be addressed in any external benefit relationship model.

**Person** is typically addressed through a mechanism of balance in the cycle of doing and being. Doing is the preference of many companies because it is closely aligned with productivity. Yet being is critical as well as it involves how employees see themselves because of their work and position. The CCO must model a balance that demonstrates a value in self and identity as well as a celebration of the work completed.

*Purpose* is a question of the humanity of the work being done by the company. The cycle of balance is between profit motive and social impact. Both are important to the employee and the community. The CCO must model how salary and community investments support family development goals and civic development goals.

*Propinquity* is a measure of engagement both in families and in the community. The balance is between pleasure and professionalism. Pleasure includes celebrations of individual effort as well as birthdays and the collective experiences such as cultural holidays. Professionalism includes human resource operations such as annual performance evaluations. The CCO communicates and manages how both pleasure and professionalism experiences are meant to inspire employees and support good will in the community.

*Perspective* concerns how people see the interactions, goals, and brand of the organization. It would seem that this is the purview of sales persons, customer service, and marketing departments, but the CCO has a seminal responsibility to communicate the ethos of place to these departments and to ensure that the integration of staff through training and professional development continues to respond to the culture of the community both internal and external.

*Systematic Implementation of Cultural Sharing*. The sharing of cultural knowledge within the company and from outside into the company must be formalized. Most effectively, this translates into structured internal / external events and processes. The CCO has the responsibility to create an ecosystem that does more than just entertain and inform, he/she must accomplish both. The additional consideration is data collection, pattern processing, and process mapping. Several means may be employed to collect, store, and disseminate this data. The main structural point is to collect, store, and disseminate in ways that encourage individual to individual interaction at every possible point in the process. Foster real interactions within context. Always debrief to see what people gain and conclude from their interactions.

## Collaboration

*Review of Cultural Vision*. Each organization has a cultural vision whether acknowledged or not. The cultural vision is the set of goals and preferred interactions that provide mutual benefit to the company and the organization most equitably. The cultural vision is one of the main deliverables of the CCO. With this presentation, the CCO sets the collaborative outcomes that are desired for the organization.

Recruitment and Retention Methods must include an assessment of the cultural vision. When companies discuss their culture and the fit of a potential employee with that culture, the cultural vision document provides a tangible starting point for team building, performance evaluation, and socially responsible activities.

*Cultural Exchange Program.* A cultural exchange program can be a useful way to explore cultures between companies / organizations. This can be an incredibly impactful method to change culture by example. When an undesirable or less than ideal cultural norm exists in an agency, cultural exchange programs can create teams with members from multiple companies. Ideally, one company has the desired culture. The CCO would coordinate the transfer of culture, balance the power dynamics, and ensure the evaluation of culture exchange. Renaissance Evolution offers a guide for such programs.

# Chapter 3: Relationship Building

Culture is best communicated through relationships. From our earliest interactions as children in a family to our most engaging work-life experiences, relationships make for effective mechanisms for culture modeling. Many fail to integrate a suitable acknowledgement of the individual in their plans for corporate functioning. The goal of corporate culture stability does not diminish the role or importance of the individual. Indeed, understanding the corporation begins with understanding the individual.

The assessment of the individual and the organization are focused primarily on opportunities for growth and development. Growth and development mean different things that different levels of ecology (individual, team, corporation, community), but the considerations are critical to mapping goals and evaluating outcomes.

Leverage and sustainability are sometimes considered only in the context of the corporation. When they include ecology and attention to relationships, the questions they answer improve employee morale, team functioning, productivity, and community good will. The energy and planning needed to maintain the work of the CCO is integrated into company functioning.

Our learning objectives in this chapter are as follows:

- Create synergy through the assessment of individual needs within the collective.
- Map the relationships that create opportunity for growth and development.
- Construct a process for scaling relationships that facilitate leverage and sustainability.

**Connecting**

From System-Wide to Individual Needs Assessment. We can get so enamored with large-scale assessment that we forget the individual component of the equation. A functional definition of the corporation that works for the Chief Cultural Officer must have an ecological systems perspective. This means that levels and actors are important to conceptualize and track operations. Levels include individual, teams, organization, and community. Actors are individuals, teams or departments, executives and spokespersons, and community officials. The additional consideration of an ecological systems perspective is that the individuals are the core unit of all the other actors. This means that they have their own individualized interpretation of any cultural add-ons resulting from the conscription of cultural norms. Because of these reactions, assessment of the individual is critical to culture transmission and culture change initiatives.

*Creating Synergy: Matchmaking*. The next logical step ecologically once individuals are engaged and assessed is to connect them in functional teams. These teams are often naturally occurring teams due to the grouping of departments or other organizational units. The CCO should be intimately involved in the hiring process at least with guidelines for hiring managers and ideally with a template for employee profiles. These profiles can be the indicators and specifications that match employees together based on important cultural information. The goal is to create the highest functioning, most creative, and complementary team.

*Understanding Application to the Collective.* Teams are not the only application to the collective. Remember that there are at least two other levels of the ecosystem: organization and community. These levels are within the purview of the CCO as well. We have discussed opportunities in the last chapter, but with relationships the main concern is how to maintain connections over time. The activities that are organized have the additional requirement to gain personal data with consent, centralize it within a customer relationship management construct, and continue engagement through both automated and intentionally personal means.

## Nodes & Networks

*Relationship Mapping.* The theoretical practice is complex adaptive systems. Know that even complex systems such as organizations made up of individuals can be mapped. Their activities, movements, and destinations can be predicted. In this case, Relationship mapping is this process of tracking the interactions between people. These interaction patterns offer a chance to predict how information will flow through the organization. Two opportunities are created through the mapping. The first is obvious as a mapping of individual interactions forms. The second is less obvious to all except organization development professionals. With individual interactions understood, you can create organizational structures that lead, invite, and influence behaviors that you desire from its members.

*Leveraging Relationships for Growth.* Behavioral economics offers an additional context for discussions on networks. The idea of influencing behavior through corporate structures, policies, and incentives is commonplace in organizations. The CCO adds to the cultural component of this discussion. Culture adds the potential to create norms that continually reinforce behaviors. The skillset of the CCO adds the ability to track, augment, and intentionally impact relationships to support certain outcomes. Each of these stages of leverage are critical to an organizational vision that engages employees, enhances outcomes, and engages the community.

*Development from Culture & Networks.* Potentially the most impactful result of a well-functioning network is the ease of information dissemination. Of course, the most important communication is the communication of culture. The additional consideration is how network functions create opportunities for education and training to occur. The process for the CCO includes personal interactions but also intentional media usage, strategic policy planning, and empowered cultural teams.

## Scaling
*Defining Relationships in terms of Scale*. Scaling is the process of taking an intervention from impact with a smaller number of people to engage a larger number. Effective scaling includes three important components: Pace, Priming, and Management. Pace describes the sweet spot, balancing the capacity available to the organization, the profit motive, and the ability to manage the implementation of the core processes at scale. Priming is a marketing activity, including all stakeholders from the board room through the vertically impacted community members. It is critical to conceptualize the priming, this broadly, to account for potentially unintended consequences and obscured opportunities. Management includes the traditional sense

of ensuring that the procedures are followed and that opportunities are followed upon. In scaling, management also includes maintaining an active system of formative and summative evaluations on a specific schedule. Trial activities, process maps, and alignment reviews are common tools in scaling management.

*Constructing Economic Sustainability*. The goal of scaling of course is economic progress and that sustainably. Contrary to the beliefs of the uninitiated, economic sustainability is more than just having a great idea. In addition to great ideas, a high functioning team, reliable supply chain, and sustained customer engagement are critical to business success. A business cannot leverage those without the ability to scale. In fact, scaling includes attention to those three concerns. The CCO is crucial to the development and structure of teams as we have discussed. The reliability of the supply chain also involves the CCO because supply chains across cultural, language, and demographic barriers must be managed to limit bottlenecks. Customer engagement during a scaling process must address the nuances of cultural exchange including how place changes the communication needs for the company. This is specific to the role and responsibility of the CCO.

*The Process of Scaling*. Once a pace, priming, and management plan is created, implementation is next. Organizational structures, team members, policies & procedures, and technology systems must be ordered and launched. Often, implementation includes consultants, temporary managers, or other partners with insight into the process, place, and people. A team of organizational development specialists will be involved in any successful scaling implementation and the CCO should be at the helm while also participating as an integral part of that team.

# Chapter 4: Disrupting One Another

The Chief Cultural Office is not a person that has the luxury of foregoing conflict. The task at hand is bolstered through the skills of operational patience, conflict resolution, and clear executional acumen, with a righteous vision. The good news is that the theoretical foundation for organizational change is well documented. The critical consideration is to resist the inclination to make the environment sterile, compliant, and competition free. In fact, the best implementation of culture change will leverage competition to its benefit. People naturally want to excel in the workplace. Use that inclination rather than fight against it. The outcome you desire is not compliance, conformity, nor political correctness. You want something more akin to loyalty or allegiance as draconian as those may sound. You want evangelists for the culture of the organization. You want stakeholders who swear by the ideals of your mission and vision themes. The process of reaching this outcome is intentional.

Our learning objectives in this chapter are as follows:
- Articulate the process of reforming, innovating, and resetting culture in organizations.
- Describe a concept of constructive competition that supports productivity and intrinsic motivation.

- Define synergy in the context of cultural disruption.

### Cultural Disruption

*Counterintuitive but Necessary.* It may be counterintuitive to consider that disruption is progress. But there are few certainties when it comes to organization development, culture change, and culture management. Cultures become entrenched as a function of great culture management AND inviting new people and cultural experiences into the organization is vital for its development and efficacious progress. Entrenchment must be loosened periodically and intentionally. Hold on to the gains in culturally connected collaboration while remaining open to innovation, novel ideas, complementary processes, and contrary opinions. Without out this intentional and periodic process, organizations become blind to their potential for innovation and ultimately blind to their own demise. In today's global business environment, you either disrupt or allow others to disrupt you.

*The Change Theory:* Schein's Culture Change theory has 3 easily comprehensible steps: Unfreezing, Cognitive Restructuring, and Refreezing. Unfreezing is the disruption that needs to take place. In this step, the status quo is questioned systematically through discussions structured to provide both recommendations and structures for continued dialogue. Cognitive Restructuring is the opportunity to educate, pattern train, and provide context to stakeholders. Recognize that the process is not just for insiders and employees. External entities including vendors and community partners are impacted by the cognitive restructuring as well. Refreezing often includes the creation of new positions and organizational structures that have the purpose of continuing to monitor or support directives that result from the culture change process.

*Resetting with Purpose*: The CCO is one of these quintessential new positions. In an organization that has already adopted the CCO position, the task is to become highly introspective. Scholars like Joseph Schumpeter suggest that the culture change be "creative destruction" where innovation impacts and replaces with insistence and permanence. A more nuanced application of the concept allows for the disruption of power as fealty to the model. This means that the CCO releases his/her power as the culture guru and guide of the organization while the process of cultural assessment and culture change resets and reforms the organizational culture in the context of mission and vision. The result is a true allowance of change, limiting the bias that exists naturally among human beings.

### Positive Competition

Defining a Perspective on Competition. Competition is not the enemy. It is a productivity / creativity tool. When used effectively, it can provide a means of external motivation. When used expertly, it can become internal motivation and sustainable choice behavior. The difference in usage begins with a novel definition that aids effective implementation of the tool.

Competition is often described as a contest between two or more people. But it has other applicable definitions. Competition can be defined as a positive and proactive reason for engaging with a problem or otherwise construed activity. Consider that competition can be the context that brings out the best in all participants. This is commonly called Positive Competition. Positive competition is competition that removes the need for an adversarial relationship. Competition can maintain its function as motivation without engendering a separative behavior or fracturing of teams.

*Connection with Culture*. Positive competition is important to culture change because cognitive restructuring is difficult work. Directives and policy imperatives are not enough to move hearts and minds. Those external motivations will need to move internally for long-term change and the type of intrinsic motivation that results in openness, team building, and collaboration. Positive competition is an effective organizational culture structure.

Implementing a positive competition structure requires soul searching and an education across multiple levels of the organization. A balance must be struck between a sense of competitive challenge with non-zero-sum calculations and the irrelevance and despair that comes from "everyone gets a trophy" approach to its implementation. It is not appropriate to have a winner-takes-all structure. It is also too simplified to have a structure that provides awards to all participants. The goldilocks structure often involves some incentive to participate in the competition that is shared by all participants and a prize that is the reward for one team or individual. For example, a positive competition structure may award an additional 30 minutes of lunch twice per week to all participants. The reward for the successful team or individual may be an additional day of vacation.

*Inspiring not Motivating.* This type of intentional structuring of intrinsic motivation supports a move from motivation to inspiration. Rather than requiring some external event or corporate action to move employees and other stakeholders to action, the ideals, values, and interests of the stakeholders themselves are engaged and allowed to connect naturally to company mission and vision. The role of the CCO is to structure environments such that this concept is more likely.

## Synergy

*Returning to Synergy.* Synergy is the end goal of every corporate intervention. Disruption is important to the process, but it is a shakeup of the status quo that must be solved prior to the completion of the process. The return to synergy will often go a step further than the refreezing stage in the change process. That change process is likely to have elements of engagement with all stakeholders, but the bulk of the focus is on organizational change and functioning. Return to synergy is a reminder to intentionally engage the community through ancillary, complementary, and external stakeholders to ensure that everyone is on the same page with desired behaviors / outcomes.

Achieving synergy is often a function of marketing campaigns and town-hall style informational gatherings. These are opportunities to present new product lines and services, but they are also opportunities to display cultural elements, practices, and perspectives. Of course, stakeholders were engaged in the process of conceptualizing these elements, practices, and perspectives. The presentation is a report out to them and a validation of their input and effort. Large scale media presentations at consumer expos, county fairs, or internally promoted health or community action days could offer a chance to accomplish this goal.

***Disruption not Dysfunction***. By following a theoretically based, evidence-based approach to organizational development, the CCO ensures that this cultural innovation experiment does not descend into chaos. The goals are clear. The releasing of power and control structure is strategic. And above all, everyone is informed continually. The perspective to take is one that builds upon the foundation of prior functioning. This engenders trust and communicates a focus on inclusion. The old ways are not bad or wrong, they are the foundation to be built upon. They are the best for that time and now must be innovated and retooled. New technology does not replace great character or good people. It allows them to extend their reach and achieve their goals more efficiently. This is the message the CCO must both champion and operationalize.

*Critical Culture & the CCO*. Several constructs of culture communication, perception, and common sense comprise an understanding of Critical Culture. Applied to organizations, critical culture is an assessment of the culture and perceptions held within an organization. But it had additional definitive features when applied by the CCO. In the hands of an expert, critical culture is like a cinematographer's shot-by-shot plan for filming a movie. The CCO can highlight and obscure the elements, processes, and power relationships as he/she sees fit. Of course, best practices suggest transparency. Effective CCO's also bring public attention to the best assets and operations and task those that lag while informing and encouraging them behind closed doors in strategy sessions. The goal is to systematically improve every aspect of the organizations culture while wisely fostering the right attention, the appropriate eyes, on the appropriate opportunities, strengths, deficits, and threats.

# Chapter 5: Seeing the Impossible as Possible

Every corporation understands that their story is their currency in the marketplace. Many have marketing departments focused night and day on communicating that story to consumers. Few recognize the need for story crafting within their organizations. Some attempt to address this need with compliance, education, and other staff development, but creation of a cultural narrative is more than simply reciting the mission. The Chief Cultural Officer can be integral in this process including the connection of the narrative to vision and actions. The CCO is also the keeper of the flame tasked with following through on the imperatives of the vision. In the execution of these duties, an effective CCO will fully demonstrate an ability to compose stories, articulate vision, evaluate mission, and align operations to logically work toward the organization's desired outcomes.

Our learning objectives in this chapter are as follows:
- Compose a narrative that supports creative thinking.
- Define innovation as a process of vision creation and breaking legacy and/or hindering protocols.
- Articulate the process of evaluating mission and outcome alignment.

## Conception (Out of the Box)

*Research on Creativity.* Corporate storytelling is not creative writing, but it does require creativity. The connection of vision to a story line, selection of case studies, metaphors, and context relationships, and more are not givens. They are the result of a solid information-based understanding of the company. Also, the result of a creative CCO.

KH Kim published her research on creativity in 2016 in her book titled *The Creativity Challenge: How to Recapture American Innovation*. Her continued research offers insight into the context of creativity for both the CCO and how the CCO structures the environment for staff and other stakeholders. Her foundational construct is that creativity incorporates climate, attitudes, and thinking. Climate is the environment and it includes; social structures, policy constraints, as well as physical spaces. Attitudes include the cultural operations, lifestyle preferences, and recreative choices. Thinking involves the capacity, openness and interactive inclinations observed. The effective CCO demonstrates awareness of each of these and an intention to influence each.

*Creating Climate is Creating Culture.* The climate component of creativity is primary for the CCO because it is the seat of culture by definition. Social structure, policies, and physical spaces make up the macro tools of the CCO. Social structures must communicate the narrative complete with plot lines, origins, and drivers. The goal is to tell a complete organizational story along with relevant / tangible experiences that can be repeated by stakeholders. Policies offer to constrain the story and keep it from becoming hyperbole. An unbelievable story is less effective because stakeholders can dismiss it as improbable. Keep the story accessible to all stakeholders. Physical spaces are great for collaboration, but they are also great places for strategic, subtle communication of the company narrative. Posters and slogans are a typical tool. Video monitors and touch screens are being used with increasing frequency as they become standard in newer or renovated building designs.

*Storytelling as a Model for Transmission of Culture.* The cornerstone of storytelling IS in the telling, the positioning, the delivery. This is also a primary concern for transmission of culture. Sharing the story with the proper inflection points, values, anecdotes and excitement can mean the difference between establishing a true connection or missing altogether. Active and intentional culture is what the CCO desires. Such a culture is useful to leverage productivity and morale.

Inflection points are the moments within the story that communicate the heroism, achievement, and moral lesson of the story. In a basic outline, this is the beginning, middle, and ending. Crafting the story with solid inflection points also aids in the communication and the eventual retelling by stakeholders. Values are the building blocks that make up the moral of the story being told. In every story, the moral lesson connects with the main character because of consistencies in that character. This allows the reader or listener to place themselves in the shoes of the character. Values are what the listener is comparing when they hear a story. The CCO will do well to connect the values of the organization within the story, with written and/or overt values promoted by the company. Excitement describes the impact of the story as it is told. Connection with the audience is the main concern. Compelling story and identifiable characters are a close second and third. The CCO must keep these in mind and craft the story creatively to achieve these goals.

### Innovation
*Visioning as a Process.* Visioning is a straightforward process

that is like storytelling except that it pulls from what is desired rather than what has occurred. Visioning begins with a conception of the ideals the company wants to see after a certain number of years. Many visioning experts suggest 5 years as a target outlook.

The next step is to create the vision themes that emerge from an analysis of the organizational vision. The outlook described by the vision should be; tangible, measurable, and specific. The CCO creates statements that will become the inflection points for the story told about the vision. When someone asks how the company achieved their goals, the vision themes reveal the process.

***Communicating the Vision through Engaging Stories***. It may be obvious that the story crafting and storytelling skills of the CCO are vital to culture communication—culture as integration within the organization. Yet the vision is the company's culture desire. This too can be communicated through storytelling. The chief concern is to create compelling stories. One of the best ways to do this is to create stories with the stakeholders at the center of the narrative. This necessarily suggests that different versions or perspectives on the story be created to service the stakeholders that are engaged by the company.

***Coopting Personnel to Tell Stories.*** The CCO must actively ensure that stakeholders are able to communicate the version of the stories that involve them. This is not just a function of ensuring dissemination. A most effective CCO will lead assessment and evaluation processes to make sure that the communication is occurring with fidelity to the desired communication.

### Evaluation

***Defining Alignment.*** Alignment between the vision and the culture of the organization is critical to both corporate success and the ability to fix any discrepancies in corporate functioning. The latter concern is the true value of alignment. One of the most challenging experiences of a company is to operate in good faith, completing good work that does not meet the expectations of stakeholders or shareholders.

***Mapping the Process, Trials, and Formative Outcomes.*** To ensure that alignment is paramount in the process, the CCO can employ the technique of mapping. Process mapping is an organizational assessment process in itself determining how things get done in the context of the organization. Process mapping can often be useful because the operations manual does not always describe the process that is occurring in the field. In Process Mapping, we create points in time where we will evaluate what is happening in a process. These are called trials. Any given organizational operation may have multiple trials. The more trials, the more specificity there is in the process mapping and the greater one's ability to make minute changes in process. When trials are integrated into the process creating the ability to make changes while the process is in operation, without having to wait for it to conclude, these are called formative changes. Formative changes can be useful with complex processes and in processes that include stakeholder feedback. The CCO will also note greater opportunity to influence culture as the formative changes are mapped.

***Aggregating for Summative Outcomes.*** Beyond formative changes, summative changes are an opportunity to take all the experiences of process under review. Formative changes are useful, but sometimes the ability to take a step back and look at the data in total can offer new insights. Aggregation is the term when the data in total is reviewed. Aggregation typically refers to combining, but in organizational evaluation, the aggregation related to the content of the review is more than the structure of the data. Aggregation can both allow for 360 review and for explanations that come through, given that all the data is available.

Of course, it is critical that data is kept in such a way that this aggregation is useful. In this manner, attention to process mapping and clear formative changes provide a data trail that supports aggregation. Data is the currency of process mapping. This data is also useful in storytelling. It undergirds the story providing evidence and punctuation to story. It is the truth hoped for in the vision and retold in the shared narrative.

# Chapter 6: Creating Greatness Together

Once story and data are secured, you have what is required to support people. What may be missing is a conception of collaboration that ensures that the structures and intent of positive competition are realized operationally person-to-person. The CCO in concert with other operators must seed vision among the employees. In effect, this is operationalizing the vision through the process map. This process must be aligned just as the vision themes and mission are themselves aligned. The end goal and external motivation for employees / members of a group, is tied to the performance evaluation process. The CCO should include cultural assessment in that process. Performance evaluation provides the external motivation, but this is only temporary. Momentum can be sustained through identification of roles and responsibilities that employees care for. The quality of life is tied to how employees see themselves as well as the work they do.

Our learning objectives in this chapter are as follows:
- Articulate the process of Seeding Vision for collaboration.
- Map a process for evaluating excellence in collaboration.
- Maintain momentum through identification of roles and responsibilities in groups.

### Seeding Vision

*Cultural Transformation Process*. The cultural transformation process involves emotions, psychology, and activities. The commitment of the organization is even more critical than the buy-in of the employees at this point. The organization communicates this commitment through a complete and end-to-end release of the organization's initiative. The affirmation extends from the top of the organization to the point of contact for employee questions and feedback. Those questions and feedback are taken seriously, integrated into change processes, and reported back to employees within short time spans, ideally within less than 7 days.

Emotional intelligence is the conception of the emotional or "winning hearts" component of the culture transformation process. The CCO must win commitment from employees on the vision laid out by the organization. Most often, this is evidenced in the actions of employees to show up, participate, and respond to processes and inquiries tied to the initiative. Be careful not to incentivize the participation as the main vehicle for motivating compliance. Long term, the CCO will want participation to extend from a true intrinsic motivation from the employee.

Psychology, or minds, refers to the knowledge base of the employees. Training is one necessary aspect of the culture transformation process. Remember that culture sharing is also an effective method. That is, create space for employees to share information and collaborate on cultural exploration together in informal ways as well as formal educational experiences. The result will support collective activities and collaborative efforts later as teams form in culture transformation projects and other projects. Typically, the resulting bonds and knowledge gained is long-term / sustainable and one that will continually produce synergy.

Activities refer to the implementation of skills developed in the culture transformation process. Practice that is without penalty is vital to the process. This is another area where informal groups can provide an opportunity for growth and experimentation. Leverage those informal groups to create opportunities for employees to make mistakes, build confidence, and practice interactions. Formal practice sessions are also warranted. These sessions can be live and/or through computer-assisted means. The live interactions allow for team building that support collaboration. The computer-assisted interactions allow for comfort and a sense that employees can make mistakes without penalty or shame. Both are important for corporate functioning.

### Excellence

*Collaborative Waypoints.* Collaboration in the organization is more than just wishful thinking. It is a science steeped in culture and theories of social development. The CCO must be explicit in the collection, packaging, and dissemination of collective activities. These are the basis for collaboration. Stated simply, collective activities are the sense that two heads are better than one. It is the shared opinion that a task can be improved by having multiple people contribute to its completion. This may be a desired norm in the organization but making it a reality is more than just desire.

*Toward a Culture of Collaboration.* The CCO truly shines in the arena of collaboration. Armed with the vision outlined, alignment protocols, process maps, and outcome directives from all areas within the organization, the CCO has all the tools to rally employees for collaboration. The trick is to construct social development protocols successfully. Such protocols rely on three considerations: platform, channels, and feedback loop.

Platform refers to the technological tool(s) used in the information sharing, team activity, and production process. The

48

platform can be tailored to fit the cultural needs of the organization. Access, information and support, interactive mechanisms, and more should be specific to the cultural intentions of the organization.

Channels refer to the ways that information is disseminated. We have discussed training and both formal and informal interaction, but channels in social development are specific conduits of culture. Think of them as television stations broadcasting culture 24/7. Consider the people, mechanisms, or implementations that can be solely dedicated to a culture of collaborative efforts. Posters, new initiatives, and new hires can encapsulate such channels.

Feedback loops are critical to the process because they demonstrate whether you are accomplishing the tasks that you set out to accomplish. They also serve another important purpose. They complete the cycle of the collaborative proposition. Sometimes, collaborative efforts can seem to focus on moving to completion without sharing best practices, formative reflections, and progress reporting with the employees who are vital to the success of the intervention. Feedback loops remind the CCO to close them and complete the cycle. The result is a well-informed employee base. This usually results in greater buy-in and increased morale.

### Maintaining Momentum

***Clear Roles & Articulated Responsibilities.*** Most companies believe that they have clear roles and responsibilities communicated through job descriptions. Many of these are the same job descriptions that were presented to the employee upon their hire. If we are honest, these are typically inadequate to describe what an employee does, let alone their role in a change initiative. The CCO will do well to take the extra effort to designate specific roles and responsibilities related specifically to the change initiative. The activities required are clear in process mapping documents. The remaining task is to parse the activities, assign them, and communicate them along with any training that is required.

*Effective Communication.* The best way to do this is to ensure the cycle of communication is perpetual. Perpetual communication has often been relegated to emails and internet postings. But today's mobile / emergent technology makes it possible to engage in real-time communication and engagement with employees. The emergence of artificial intelligence enables real-time, natural-speaking interactions with employees. If available, the CCO should utilize these technologies to go beyond the information dissemination function. Surveys, priming, invitations, and teaming can be facilitated through technologies. This frees the CCO to coordinate broad-stroke and foundational structures.

*Centralized Information & Culture.* The first consideration is reminiscent of marketing and storytelling. Centralizing information is not just about controlling the narrative. It is about ensuring that the flow of information is continual. The second consideration is about how the information is utilized. It must be used to spur momentum. Utilize the information flow, the engine created through attention to perpetuate effective communication. Continue to contribute to the knowledge and information sourced from all stakeholders. Keep employees informed about the community impact as well as the corporate intention. The result is an employee that feels personally responsible for the corporate initiatives and the impact in the communities where it conducts business.

# Chapter 7: Shaping Evolution in the Global Economy

Jose Rodriguez, Chief Strategy & Development Officer for Renaissance Evolution, presents the proposition succinctly:

*"Global corporations can lead the change towards establishing a truly reciprocal and symbiotic relationship between business and culture."*

*"A true balance of business operations and global social responsibility can go hand in hand in making a corporation more profitable while differentiating it from others in its category. The institution of the Chief Cultural Officer will ensure that corporations reduce government dependence and leave a tangible positive footprint in the markets and countries where they operate. The goodwill generated will have a multiplier effect in terms of its brand, market expansion as well as increased earnings.*

*This complete view of the company and its global,*

*national, and regional operations as well as its understanding of the local cultures and leading community / political figures in markets represented will in fact position him/her as a corporate ambassador. Much like a Secretary of State or Minister of Foreign Affairs, The Chief Cultural Officer will ensure that a company's global approach to business is market relevant, profitable, and sustainable.*

Today it is easy to engage and/or plan to conduct business at a global level. However, the cultural complexities and intricacies of relating in a "smaller" world are many times unseen, misunderstood or even worse, completely ignored. Unfortunately, not everyone is simply capable of relating or of thriving in a global environment. If people (human capital), the engines that power companies experience difficulties with relationship-building, diversity, innovation and an overall open mind to the new economy requirements of constant re-invention, flexibility, acceptance and a hunger to truly connect with others - maximum business potential is not achieved. In addition, if individuals are not given the necessary training or do not share in such a vision, then the organization as a whole will inevitably suffer. What are seemingly insignificant and considered to be personal rather than collective or organizational attributes are truly critical factors for conducting business and scalable growth. However, because these attributes are considered to be second nature and simple in terms, many business, political and diversity curriculums do not focus enough on this basic set of skills and how they impact / weave into the DNA of organizational culture and operations.

At the end of the day, business IS very personal and those not able to make multi-level connections with counterparts, who possess exclusive rather than inclusive agendas, that operate in a vacuum without concern for rules, ethics or individuals will inadvertently hinder the operations of a global organization. It is important to note that the individual is mostly not at fault for lacking the proper vision or tools to execute. Many times, legacy corporate cultures and the repetition of learned (even if incorrect) behavior and strategies are the genesis of such organizational "bad habits".

Organizations seeking "good success" and growth must take time and dedicate resources through constant evaluation of their processes. Just because something worked yesterday doesn't mean that it will work today or that there won't be a better way of doing it tomorrow. Adaptability, fluidity, understanding and empathy - a certain type of "cultural camouflage" - that can be applied to any organization, is the true art of connecting and positively influencing others to collective success.

Conducting business, is nothing more than a natural extension of such interpersonal behavior. Sure, the bottom-line must not be ignored. After all, business without profit is not an option.

However, ROI is not the only measure of success nor the only reason for a business to operate or an organization to exist. The business or organization must fill a need and in order to receive the support of others, those who are a part of it must holistically represent the persona of that group as well as keenly focus on the void it fills, regardless of whether it is a product or service. It is through the operational / culture lens of the Chief Cultural Officer and methodology that an organization's message should be crafted and disseminated. It is through a network of equally vested individuals that a global community and movement is built.

This is how you innovate, how you lead, how you disrupt, how you inspire, how you scale and how you succeed in an ever fluid global economy. Ultimately and as an organic result of applying this methodology, the organization will be positively impacted / equipped to succeed over its competitors and as a natural bi-product, be able to reach its initial goal of becoming highly profitable".

Our learning objectives in this chapter are as follows:
- Map global trends in the context of cultural competence and the ability to positively leverage those environments.
- Apply concepts of Learning, Economics, and Impact in the context of cultural diversity. "Cultural Camouflage"
- Scaffold a movement based in culture, language, and diversity for economic & social benefits.

### Renaissance Evolution Academy

Economic interactions between businesses and consumers are characterized by diversity in; country of origin, cultural background, political structure and stability, as well as economic history and its prognosis. Diversity and complexity are the norms. Understanding how to approach and cohesively apply inclusive business practices that allow seamless navigation of the new and continually evolving business diversity issues are key in the successful operation and expansion of companies. A holistic approach will position our Chief Cultural Officer candidates to successfully become the multinational face both internally and externally for its corporation. This new C-Level position will interact with internal divisions of Government Affairs, Diversity, Communications, Strategy, Human Resources, Financial, Operations and others with direct impact on the corporate profits and losses.

### Global Trends

*Trend Mapping.* The year 2020 has witnessed an unforeseen level of global change impacting corporate functioning including staffing patterns and cultural considerations. This is only the latest, and possibly the most revolutionary of global trends. Without spending too much time lamenting the incredible disruption of the COVID-19 pandemic, the takeaway for organizations is that extreme disruption can be an opportunity to conceptualize novel ways to do everything within an organization.

Other trends are far less disruptive, but no less important to map. In trend mapping, the goal is to look for opportunities based in the perception of employees, customers, and other stakeholders. The reports about trends should be specifically insightful and tied to identified populations. Insights can then be applied intentionally to those specific populations. The CCO is critical to the interpretation and implementation of these reports because they are specifically looking for cultural indicators that signal an ability to leverage culture for corporate gains.

**Constructing a Cultural Observation List.** The core consideration assisting the interpretation and implementation of the trend report is the Cultural Observation List. This list is constructed based on the cultural analysis of the corporation, context including place, and the vision and mission alignment of the corporation. Items on the list are like the items included in performance evaluations. The difference is that these concepts are listed in an ecologically relevant table. This means that they are conceptualized at all levels of operations within the company. For example, at the micro/employee level, you have the performance evaluation. At the manager level, you have the performance targets. At the senior manager level, you have the management parameters and outcome metrics. At the C-level, you have the shareholder value reporting metrics. The CCO monitors each of these constructing a list of indicators that respond to cultural matters like a weathervane for corporate functioning and opportunity.

*What to Compare.* You can compare the standard department profile, but this may not provide as much insight as breaking the community up into clusters based on shared movements. Track those who use the cooler at the same time, those who go out for lunch versus those who stay in the break room, who clock in at the same time, who take advantage of recreation, who create biking groups, and more.

### Considerations in Application: Learning, Economics, and Impact

Application of the Cultural Observation List is best conceptualized as a logical process that connects learning, economic value, and impact to the activities of the CCO. The CCO becomes the proxy for cultural functioning in the organization. This designation is a construct beyond the position itself to not only operationalize the role, but to effectively wield culture in the organization as a tool for growth and development.

*Learning and Culture.* We have discussed training and development in previous chapters. What may add value here is to discuss the challenges in implementation that may occur. More than the challenges along for consideration, the perspective best used for interpretation of the challenges and solutions is a critical consideration. The CCO should always view culture as an interactive process. That means that instead of seeing antagonists and protagonists, the CCO sees actors with agendas and desired outcomes. Learning should always be structured to inform the agendas and offer alignment for the desired outcomes. Transparency is not just about meetings and showing what the corporate goals are... It is about connecting the goals of the individual with the goals of the corporation. This is best accomplished by engaging the individual to create goals that align with the corporation. Follow up with these to ensure that the individual is empowered to use the tools at hand to articulate themselves and comprehend the position and imperatives of the corporation.

*Economics and Culture.* Profit and loss are the baseline metrics of the corporation. But they are not always the end-all from a corporate functioning and morale point of view. The CCO must marry the economics of the balance sheet with the economics of culture. This is best accomplished through an understanding of behavioral economics. The general idea we have discussed is how to support behaviors desired by the corporation. The additional consideration is the CCO can calculate the financial benefit of individual behaviors. A simple example is to measure the cost of hiring an employee compared to the cost of retaining an employee. Engaging culture change to support a healthy work environment has financial returns that can support profit growth.

*Impact and Culture.* Logically, impact is the result of the outcome that is felt and creates perception among stakeholders. The CCO is not only concerned with operations and feedback. CCO's are concerned with the impact that is felt. Contrary to the musings of some, the CCO must develop metrics that coincide with impact for stakeholders. Examples may include number of attendees to community events, amount of corporate giving, positive interactions with stakeholders, and other indicators that are important even if not traditionally directly tied to the balance sheet.

### Continuous Learning through Renaissance Evolution
*Structuring a Movement.* A movement requires leadership, content for training, and an evaluation structure. In addition to these as internal initiatives, organizations can benefit from external consultancies that provide expertise and a level of advanced tutelage

for executives and managers. Implementation of the CCO methodology could benefit from such a consultancy's offerings. Renaissance Evolution Academy is one such consultancy / source of future CCO's.

*Mobilizing Champions.* The model of the movement begins with identification of champions in the creation of culture change within the organization. The CCO is a C-Suite position because this level of engagement provides the internal knowledge, access and leadership required. This project represents the content for training the CCO. The evaluation structure is best created in concert with the performance evaluation process already in operation within the organization.

Renaissance Evolution (RE) intends to effect positive development traits that in turn can minimize the general population's dependency on government aid or intervention, helping to create a more sustainable and happier modern society via the interaction of highly engaged corporations.

RE is keenly aware of the direct economic and cultural impact of global business in the markets where investments and operations are executed. Given this direct correlation, it is one of the goals of RE to ensure that commercial / operational practices of multinational companies are socially responsible and offer a sustainable balance that allows not only the financial growth of these companies, but also the same within the communities where they conduct business.

International trade is the standard and will continue to shape our daily lives. Every day the world becomes smaller and more interdependent, to the point where seemingly trivial corporate decisions may have tremendous and sometimes unimaginable effects on people around the globe.

An understanding of human culture, its influence on business and their collective place in history can help build a better future. RE proposes to develop a new international business culture to serve as the foundation that promotes the kind of corporate core values and vision that promote a civil conscience in people of all nations. This concept is about embracing; reciprocity, transparency, responsibility, empathy, and sustainability in business, while still positively impacting the commercial bottom-line.

# Section II: 8 Pillars For Sustainable Global Influence

# Chapter 8: Learning Pillars

## Pillar 1: Culture & Education

It is not enough to be culturally sensitive. Cultural education is critical. The challenge is that many believe that education is the simple presentation of information. With cultural discussions, the reality is more than presentation of information. It is engagement and expression that facilitates exchange, education, and experience. The goal of culture and education is appreciation, even celebration, of the culture.

Culture exchange is most effectively completed through a process including guided interaction within a specific, identifiable context. The guide, the interaction, and the context are crucial to creating the opportunity for sustainable exchange. Culture guides are often insiders within the culture. They may be people who grew up in the culture or who have adopted the culture as their own through immersion. A guide both has experience with the culture and enough of a relationship with the learner to correct / inform behaviors. Interactions are free from judgment in either direction.

The negotiation of culture that may be observed in a new friendship is replaced with a navigation of cultural norms that accepts behaviors as rules rather than preferences to be questioned. For exchange to be most effective, this acceptance should commence without resistance initially even as questions are welcome. The context must be one where the culture is continually presented and reflected upon by the learner.

An example would be when the language of the culture is spoken exclusively. This causes the learner to process without their typical cues and comfort. Such a disorientation and need for guided navigation supports opportunities for identification and appreciation of differences.

Education that occurs within this exchange process is obvious. It includes exposure to language and customs. It can be delivered in a classroom setting, but will necessarily require some elements of culture exchange to be most effective. The curriculum must include language training and custom exploration presenting an exploration of the diversity of people and place.

Language training is not always limited to presentations resulting in speaking ability. The cadence, tonality, and history of the language can provide a foundation for appreciation. Even the ability to recognize the language when spoken, differentiating from other languages can be a positive step toward appreciation. Language is critical because communication is central to education. Custom exploration refers to considerations of the daily habits of culture. These may include food consumption and preparation, activity schedules, and hopes and dreams for the future. Practicing or exploring these provide a window into the daily life of a people. Questions about where people find themselves during the day, their approach to time and place, their posture toward one another and more are matters of custom.

Experience is most sustainably provided in context. For example, programs that offer the opportunity for learners to live with a family (full cultural immersion) are the most effective option. The daily interactions create opportunities for culture exchange that are difficult to approximate without the immediate vicinity functions. The experience often termed culture shock is useful in the context of culture and education. This means that the learner has experienced a separation from known codes, cues, and contexts and must navigate a new environment without those anchors. It is advisable to have some anchor in known codes, cues, and contexts to ensure that the learner is not overwhelmed, but suspending those lifelines is appropriate. For example, calls home from the cultural experience abroad could be confined to one day per week or limited to an hour per day.

Similar strategies could translate into business practices that respect the culture through a deep knowledge and appreciation. It is more than a simple awareness of culture or recitation of customs. It is an ability to place oneself under the jurisdiction of a new culture, to navigate its requirements, and find value. The resulting appreciation of the other and the culture is enhanced.

## Pillar 2: Health / Well-being & Happiness

Areas of diversity create a scenario where the messenger is just as important as the message. Diversity areas include gender, religion, age, ethnicity, language, and ability. There may be opportunities for universal messaging, but there is no question that the sense and definition of health and well-being is different from different areas of diversity. For example, women may construct different definitions of health and well-being than men. Older individuals may see things different from younger individuals. Those of faith may have different priorities than those with other faiths. With this in mind, the central goal of Health, Well-being & Happiness is to ensure that people who represent the target population are hired to interact with those constituents whenever possible.

The deep strength and capability of any group is the diversity of thought that is included in the group. What we mean by this is to highlight the fact that thinking is the foundation of our cultural difference engine. Representation is not just about checking off our diversity buttons. It must be about engaging individuals who hold a context, origination, and process rooted in a cultural experience different from that already present within the team. Context here refers to the mental space created when a concept or process is considered. Contexts are necessarily different for individuals who speak different languages, have different cultural experiences, and more. Tapping into this context rather than attempting to conform to an expected context is a skill worth cultivating. Managers must strive to create these open and affirming contexts for thought.

Origination here refers to the starting point of thoughts and ideas. Origin is unique to each individual but may be influenced by expected or conformed patterns of thinking based in education and/or routine. Origination answers the question, "Where does your mind go when considering this concept or problem?" For everyone, the origination often begins with who they see themselves to be. This includes a consideration of their role but also may (hopefully) include culture. Process is the way people execute their daily tasks. A most common routine in business is the consumption of coffee in the morning. Simple variations include how people take their coffee or whether they skip coffee altogether in favor of tea or another beverage. Process signals a routine but also a point of departure like origination. The difference is that process is directly related to behaviors that offer a point of commonality or potential valued difference among individuals on a team.

These differences, like diversity considerations, can sometimes offer a greater need for translation. Hence, patience, perseverance, and policy must support continued communication even if it is mediated. Rather than penalizing and hiding difficulties, an approach toward restorative justice can be fruitful. Restorative justice allows for transparent communications about the challenges, proposed solutions, and ongoing training around those interventions.

Health, well-being, and happiness are connected through the representation of the group. That is, the diversity of the group offers multiple expressions and experiences of health, well-being, and happiness. Organizations do well to explore these varying expressions and experiences as attention to them create the opportunity for validation, cheerleading, and support of individuals on the team. For example, honoring birthdays, holidays, and recreation activities may increase a sense of job satisfaction and create a healthier work environment.

## Pillar 3: Transparency & Ethics

More than the desires of the few, transparency and ethics refer to the insistence on the common good. The central challenge here is to create this cultural pillar with both the specificity of a rule-based structure and the flexibility that invites individual deviations from the established norm. The goal must be focused on creating the boundaries of the culture rather than prescriptions of the culture. In addition, the communication of the boundaries as policy must promote interaction rather than stifling discourse. Stated more simply, the goal is to support creativity within identified bounds of culture and promote interactive and ongoing communication as a cultural norm.

Boundaries offer a playing field for everyone to operate within.

As opposed to prescriptions that suggest a maze to be navigated, boundaries suggest an array of options available to everyone. This is the proverbial level playing field that many equity and inclusion professionals talk about. The field should not only be level but should be in full view of everyone involved. No area should be obscured. Every actor should be able to view and access options that are common to all.

Communication is critical to success. Yet organizations often hold policies or informal procedures that stifle the communication required for progress and the flow of culture throughout the organization. The result may be misunderstandings rooted in missed and incomplete communications. When these are regarding methods, behaviors, or beliefs centered in culture, opportunities for greater appreciation and productivity may be missed. For example, a worker may be annoyed that the end of year celebration is called a holiday party rather than a Christmas party. Transparency suggests that the naming convention and reasoning be shared among employees. When a CEO or similar official makes a statement valuing the varied cultural traditions represented within the company, the worker who was once annoyed may be inspired to realize that more than Christian traditions may be practiced at his/her place of employment. Rather than hiding religious discussions, the company may promote an understanding of differing traditions even without singling out any one employee.

# Chapter 9: Economic Pillars

## Pillar 4: Business for Good

Business for Good is at the intersection of social movement and corporate philanthropy. On the social movement side, the questions concern the level and extent of the intervention. On the philanthropy side, the questions concern methods of giving and level of contribution. The goal with Business for Good is to bring together social movement and corporate philanthropy to address identified challenges in areas of relevance to the organizational vision and/or mission. The identified challenges in the context of culture relate to learning, economics, and impact.

Social movements take four forms that explain the extent of intervention: Alternative, Redemptive, Reformative, and Revolutionary. Alternative movements focus on individual behavior change that is self-directed. Redemptive movements focus on changes that are typically of a spiritual nature. Like alternative movements, they are individualized. Reformative movements target a specific aspect of social policy, that are limited in scope but propose important or significant changes for groups of individuals. Revolutionary movements are large-scale and far-reaching social change propositions. They may begin with more targeted intervention but always have intentional scale potential. Business for Good likely targets reformative and revolutionary movements in the context of business goals.

Corporate philanthropy has been a fixture of corporate identity since the 1980s. Corporations make their contributions to society in multiple ways. It may be through donation of work hours, employee service days, event sponsorships, or direct financial contributions. The most important outcome is the impact on society that results from the philanthropy.

Combining social movements with corporate philanthropy has caught on in corporate policy and social enterprise designations like Benefit Corporations or B-Corps for short. Becoming a B-Corp is a matter of receiving the designation after consideration by the review committee. Corporations who want to do good are encouraged to perform actions, structure their governance, and report their revenue in ways that support the transparency, social commitment, and sustainability propositions outlined in the B-Corp review criteria.

## Pillar 5: Sustainability

The word sustainability is used often in corporate discussions today. It is used to describe everything renewable from recycling to digital paperwork. Most scholars categorize sustainability into three principles: economic, social, and environmental. The goal of this pillar is to promote corporate responsibility. Yet this is not your 1980s corporate responsibility. This version of sustainability addresses the economic sustainability for the company in terms of profits and growth trends. It addresses social interests through its community impact and its talent acquisition and development. It addresses environmental sustainability in carbon footprint, pollution, packaging, waste disposal, and a host of other considerations. Some speak of these concerns as money, people, and planet.

Money concerns are a natural consideration of companies. The bottom line of the balance sheet is what signals the health of the company. Yet companies are realizing that their cultures are what drives the bottom line. With this understanding, the consideration shifts from margins and profit making to include a consideration of the investments a company makes to achieve its goals. Market trends continue to be a consideration. But added to this concern is an environmental scan and consumer research to determine whether the company is meeting the needs it intends to meet.

People concerns are related to the monetary concerns as companies determine how to invest in their employees. Training is a typical intervention, but social events, wellness, and recreational programs are also viable options. Companies recognize the impact on health and wellbeing when a culture of communication, activity, and work-life balance is fostered. The secondary result of such attention is talent luring as the company becomes more attractive as an integrated component of a healthy life. Companies are likely to include recreation on site, free and healthy snacks, ergonomic workstations, and even on-premise childcare in some cases.

The Planet will conjure visions of global warming responses in the minds of many. Yet the interventions suggested as environmental responsibility must also be economically wise. Implementation of solar and other renewable technologies, skylights for natural lighting of spaces, utilization of recycled materials, and a host of other technologies save money / resources while inspiring its labor force to do the same in their personal lives.

## Pillar 6: Trade / Economic Opportunity

Trade equals trust and familiarity. Economic opportunity provides for the accumulation of capital that is the foundation of generational economic growth. Economic independence is the vehicle for success in corporations as well as societies. The goal with trade and economic opportunity is to create a foundation for wide-ranging impact.

Mechanisms of trust are easy to comprehend when you recognize that people are more collaborative when their purposes align. When purpose signals goals that are congruent, people look out for other's interest and as a natural correlate to monitoring and ensuring their own interests. This leverage of what may seem self-interest is the foundation of human behavior at work. Human beings are beset with an instinctual drive toward self-preservation. This individual need extends to corporate behavior no matter how large the organization or nation state.

The more a collaborative party understands the needs of the other party, the more predictable and reciprocal the behavior. This familiarity results in expectation of behavior. No matter the preference or compatibility, familiarity provides comfort. When the predicted behavior aligns with the purposes of both parties, familiarity combines with trust to create collaborative opportunity.

People cannot advance without economic opportunity. Without the economic advancement of its people, corporate bodies nor nation states can prosper. Stability and progress are a function of economic independence. Complete independence may not be possible in the short term, but the closer the individual, organization, or state gets to such independence, the more autonomous they become.

This reality offers an important context for the Chief Cultural Officer. Economic opportunity is not just about the base salary communicated in hiring documents. The opportunity for financial literacy, empowerment, and inclusion can also be a central component of economic opportunity at individual, family, group, organization, and state levels. Financial literacy refers to the basic economic principles informing learners about the markets and market processes. For example, the CCO may sponsor training about household budgeting with the intention to help employees manage their finances. Financial empowerment is providing assets for individuals to participate in financial markets. For example, the CCO may advocate for wage packages that relate specifically to the needs of workers in a specific locale. Wage packages that include gym membership, recreation allowances, or additional time on lunch breaks may fit better for a certain culture. Financial inclusion is the provision of advanced mechanisms for participation in financial markets. For example, the CCO may champion the employee stock purchase plan of the corporation knowing that financial advancement supports healthy, loyal employees.

A further discussion commences in later pillars, but the impact of economic and mutually beneficial relationships cannot be overestimated. This is especially true in the context of its promise to create global impact. Within organizations, this environment offers greater productivity as collaborative activity, financial well-being, and positive expectations support a sustainable organizational culture.

# Chapter 10: Global Impact Pillars

## Pillar 7: Diplomacy & Peace Building

The foundation created by the other pillars is leveraged within the global impact pillars of Diplomacy & Peace Building as well as Foreign Policy. Diplomacy & Peace building speak to the communication, brokering, and stabilization that results from intentional corporate citizenship and the management of culture that the CCO champions. The goal is enhanced communication, brokering of community benefit, and stabilization of environments. Each of these is a boon for the organization as they provide a solid foundation for the growth of a consumer base.

### Communication

Communication in this pillar is not a simple sender-receiver relationship. Enhanced communication is the intention to get people talking that may not have been in conversation with one another. It is to get people at the table or enlarge the table to include parties that have strategic importance to the community. Notice, the driver is not the goals of the organization. The driver must be the benefit to the community. Secondarily, the benefits are reaped by the organization, but that prioritization is critical to the success of the endeavor for three reasons: champions, change, and sustainability.

Champions are those in the community who have worked to establish a voice or those who the organization can support to expand their voice. They are also often key informants that can educate the organization on the history, status, and ethos of the community. In this way, they become valuable spokespersons for the integration of organization and community needs. They also become voices of reason during disputes and conflict. Identifying these individuals is most often done through an informal survey of community individuals. Random contacts, when asked for their top 5 people to connect with in the community, will give you your champions within that top 5. The order may differ from person to person, but the list will be more similar as you ask around.

Change requires champions to perform the functions listed above in exercise of their voice. It is also important to recognize the nature of change itself in the context of communication. Formulation, repetition, and reinforcement are crucial. Formulation must be in the language and context of the community. Champions can help to create and revise organizational messaging. They are your primary focus group. Repetition comes through an informal, word-of-mouth marketing that champions are vital in executing. They know where, when, and how best to disseminate information such that it becomes the talk of the town. Reinforcement is a significant tool of learning. Just short of expansion of ideas, reinforcement is ensuring that the reasoning behind the message is clear and the that expansion has a foundation of understanding.

Sustainability here refers to the longevity of messages. Once a change is initiated in the voice of champions and the context of a change model, the new normal created must be maintained. Often, the best way to do this is through print messaging placed throughout the community in key locations. These may be magazines, billboards, posters, or commercials depending on the ways that the community receives and digests information. Champions may also give way to ambassadors who carry on scheduled conversations with the community sustaining the message of the organization. This is more than propaganda. It is also a feedback loop from which the organization can collect information about how the community is responding to the communications.

### Brokering

Organizations have a responsibility centered in an opportunity to define community. Most effectively, this is executed with the help of community key informants or champions. But importantly, the economic, civic, and climate impact by the organization is integral to any definition. In short, the fact that the organization is present changes the definition of the community. An effective CCO ensures that this definition is for the benefit of the newly defined community.

Economically, the gold standard is reciprocity. Everything that is provided by the workers, auxiliaries, and supporters of the organization must be matched with benefit in some form initiated from within the organization. For workers, this often means a livable wage that responds to the needs they have daily. It also may include benefit packages including work hours, vacations, leave allowances, work environments, training, and family supports that uniquely, even individually, respond to their needs. It is not uncommon to see a wholly different work reality in different locales responding to the place.

Civic impact is primarily made possible through donations. Money is a typical currency, but it is not the only currency. Donation of space, speakers, and other in-kind offerings can go a long way toward civic impact. The critical consideration is of the community's value against the community's interests. The effort is toward providing the greatest impact in the most direct implementation.

Climate is a function of the reality created by the organization's presence. When this is done poorly, the organization is an eyesore, annoyance, and a source of frustration. When done correctly, the organization is a natural extension, even a defining feature, of the community. You see the latter when towns embrace the organization and build complementary businesses, recreation, and green spaces in support of a new community definition. Of course, organizations can contribute personnel hours, in-kind donations, and funds to these efforts.

**Stabilization**

Corporations bring a wealth of knowledge in at least two ways to discussion of peace and security. First, they bring the experience of navigating culture within their organizations. Secondly, they bring the first-hand knowledge of creating peace proactively as a matter of culture rather than waiting to respond to conflict. The Chief Cultural Officer is at the forefront of this expertise.

When applied correctly, navigating culture within the organization is a microcosm of the surrounding community. Hires incorporate local workforce representatives and employees from other locales. This provides an opportunity for cultural exploration, appreciation, and often conflict resolution. In the process cultural understanding may foster the creation of a new experience for the other.

Cultural exploration is best initiated with culture guides sharing aspects of their culture. This authentic, first-hand presentation of value provides an emotionally relevant view of culture that is difficult for any standard training to capture. The opportunity for community is actualized as officers from the organization bring the practical expertise and intentional action to board rooms, volunteer events, and corporate sharing events with real people in their daily spaces.

## Pillar 8: Foreign Policy

Foreign policy is the natural progression of organizational impact and culture exploration. Most importantly, organizations must resist the inclination to replicate a dominant or comfortable culture onto the template of the host culture. The transaction is not a negotiation either. Appreciation of the host culture requires that it is the standard by which any changes are judged. The process is one of assessment, benefit analysis, and integration. The goal is to create policies that address the economic opportunity, promote business goals, and provide ongoing education and training. These are standard policy change elements. They are also solid business practices that a CCO can champion in the halls of the organization as well as city halls and government congresses.

Assessment of policy is critical to organizational functioning at the basic levels. Policies regarding origination, taxation, and human resources are mainstays of corporate functioning and business practice. Other policies regarding civic, local, and cultural matters is of equal importance as they inform personnel interactions. Benefit analysis refers to a more targeted assessment of the connections and opportunities for cultural leverage within the policies both de jure and de facto. Cultural leverage may be regarded as opportunities to achieve the business-supporting goals of the organization with the typical processes embedded within a culture. A simple example is the idea of siesta in some Latin cultures. Productivity is increased with a balanced workday. Leveraging the cultural norm of a break midday can boost productivity of teams performing in that culture. Integration is the intentional implementation of business-supporting cultural practices into the culture of the organization. More than leveraging, this practice creates policy within the organization based on culture observed outside the corporation.

Economic Policy. The originating question here was covered earlier. That was, people are influenced when their basic needs for sustainability are met. As a matter of foreign policy, we expand the scope of this influence and monitor the impact on health and well-being resulting from the exchange. Here, we focus on the economics of financial markets and exchange but also the economics of barter and relationship. When reciprocity is integrated as a matter of policy in an ecological way, exponential outcomes are possible.

Financial markets and exchanges extend as business operations commence. The most important aspects here are typical with any market exchange: customer satisfaction and margins. Customer satisfaction as a matter of culture includes wording and ethos as well as the common marketing considerations of audience, repetition, and brand messaging. Wording most famously was communicated in the debacle of the Chevy Nova introduced in Spanish-speaking markets. Of course, No Va (NO GO) in Spanish is not what you would want to communicate about a vehicle. Ethos can also be explained using the same example. The case study of the Chevy Nova also emphasizes the need to explore a market to understand what they value in branding. The name is a convention for marketing or organization or product line identification. But it can also be a message to consumers. Constructing naming conventions that fit with the culture of place may be a marketing boon resulting in sales and loyalty.

Margins are historically simple profit calculations. In the context of culture and foreign policy, they also include an assessment of the quality of life proposed for the consumers within a certain market. A brilliant case study is the focus of Walmart in the United States. Low prices are an important message within that market. Yet another important consideration is the *Made in America* branding. Together, especially in certain subsections of the United States market, the idea of supporting local businesses even while being a multi-national conglomerate are important to communicate. As a result, in these markets, purchasing, distribution, and pricing may have a different margins target. The point is not just to maximize profits, but to respect the culture of place and the sensitivities of the consumers within the market subset. Just like stocking the shelves with products that customers want to buy, Chief Cultural Officers would train advise on inventory protocols that speak to the concerns of customers.

Reciprocity is simply the consideration of value received on both sides of any transaction. In the context of culture and foreign policy, this is best communicated as a matter of corporate citizenship. Sponsorship of community events that support a common mission or value proposition are the most common implementation of this reality. A further expression of this may be found in the creation of place. A good example of this may be with corporations that take up the cause of a community to bolster its economic viability. Whirlpool Corporation and its adoption of the Benton Harbor/St. Joseph Michigan community is a notable example. This type of corporate citizenship is not just about sponsorship and financial donations. It includes strategic building of factories and office space, creation of green spaces, and corporate housing that provides a tax base and beautification for a community.

*Business Promotion*. Leveraging the reciprocity and good will of the community, business is promoted as a matter of community identity rather than marketing to sustain a brand identity. This is not to say that the marketing budget is suspended. It often means that marketing dollars are used in different ways. A common example is to connect corporate identity and community promotion with business promotion goals. Many companies are not afraid of taking sides in the current age of business practice. Recent examples include Hobby Lobby's CEO letter expressing corporate values or Oreo brand support through rainbow colored, multiple filling in their classic cookie. Marketing that connects with target communities connects with geographic communities and social communities.

*Education & Training.* Training is critical to supporting vibrant corporations. Without a viable workforce with the skills to perform the job tasks, the corporation fails. Therefore, corporations are the greatest driver of community education efforts. They accomplish this through community fairs that extend their employee training into practice. The idea is that learning in the classroom is important, but practice in the field with real clients is invaluable to learning.

# About the Author

Roberto Masiero is a business and international relations expert par excellence! With an impressive resumé of experience validating the afore statement. Dr. Masiero is the Executive Director of Renaissance Evolution, a non-partisan/non-profit, market-friendly think tank based in Washington D.C, operating in the Education and public policy space with international reach.

As Founder of Renaissance Evolution Dr. Masiero has developed a new methodology to collaborate with leading international academic institutions, governments, and private sector in the dissemination of the Chief Cultural Executive Officer curriculum.

Roberto is also expert advisor for digital, telecom, cybersecurity, and cleantech sectors. He is a recognized expert in government relations, business strategy, and media marketing strategy.

Due to his active interest in the community and endless list of participation for the good of the public, Roberto is considered an important liaison fomenting valuable lines of communication between the United States and Italy, Central America, and South America.

# Endorsements

---

### **Dr. Anthony J. DeNapoli**
*Dean of International Affairs*
*Nova Southeastern University*

Dr. Masiero lays out a clear, concise and compelling reason for organizations and institutions to consider creating the position of Chief Cultural Officer. Now more than ever we need to think strategically about how to promote global competence and effectively promote cross cultural teams. The CCO will play a key role in developing the vision and the effective implementation of a much-needed organizational culture shift.

### **Daniel Garza**
*President of Libre Initiative and Former Associate Director of the Office of Public Liaison in the White House*

Masiero has proposed a fresh and innovative approach to the world of business. Adapting to change, adding value to an organization, and anticipating customer trends can all be improved with the right team in place - and consideration of a company's culture should be front and center to assure success.

### **Victoria Fassrainer**
*Author & International Affairs Specialist*

The sections on the role of cultural disruption are particularly compelling, in addition to the overall emphasis on the general of the individual in the broader corporate ecosystem. I look forward to seeing C-Suites integrate the important role of CCO.

## Dale V.C. Holness
*Mayor of Broward County, Florida*

Broward County was thrilled to introduce the innovative concept of the Chief Cultural Officer at our 2019 Florida International Trade and Cultural Expo (FITCE) uniting leaders and business delegations from 60 countries around the world. The role of the Chief Cultural Officer in a corporation should be universal and is of much significance in today's global landscape as it helps businesses better comprehend the impact and outcome of people-to-people relationships on their success

## Paola Isaac Baraya
*Economic Development Specialist – International Trade, Broward County Office of Economic and Small Business Development*

As an educator for international trade via our 11 Steps to Exporting program, we try to instill the importance of fostering trust and relationship-building as strategies to conquer new international markets. The Chief Cultural Officer represents the personification of this philosophy and every business should consider creating this role in their organization as a key to success.

## John Wensveen, Ph.D.
*Chief Innovation Officer & Executive Director*
*NSU Broward Center of Innovation*
*Nova Southeastern University*
*Alvin Sherman Library, Research, and Information Technology Center*

We are in an age of disruption and acceleration resulting in rapid change on a global scale. The future is "now" and Dr.

Masiero's book is timely as it addresses the need for corporations to rethink what they do which includes a cultural shift focused on eight pillars. The role of the Chief Cultural Officer is impactful acting as the bridge between external and internal audiences resulting in successful execution of the vision. This book is a great read for senior leadership as it will capture your attention and create opportunities to think differently and be ahead of the curve when it comes to change and successful outcomes.

## The Honorable Pier Ferdinando Casini
## Member of the Italian Senate and former President of the Italian Chamber of Deputies

This volume explores with great insight and clarity how the figure of the Chief Cultural Officer (CCO) can guarantee each company a more modern and global approach capable of ensuring development and growth.

In these pages, Roberto Masiero reveals himself as profound observers of the contemporary business world, highlighting the importance of a rigorous knowledge of cultural evolution. Indeed, if the prevailing culture is the place of values that shape consumer attitudes, "extracting" that culture to arrive at those values cannot fail to be an imperative in strategic planning.
Taking inspiration from the eight pillars described in the book, the CCO is presented as a sort of "Corporate Ambassador" capable of redesigning relationships both internally and externally, monitoring and disseminating change.

Only with a CCO that has authority and responsibility, in fact, will an organization be able to create and sustain a vibrant and thriving business capable of reading the changes in society's tastes and preferences and recognizing new models.

Making the concepts of collaboration and participation our own, through close and frequent connections between the different levels of the structure, is one of the winning keys to follow the flow of transformational innovation that we live today, especially since the digital age has redefined the organization. of work at management level not only in companies with a strong technological vocation.

An indispensable guide for those wishing to pursue a career as a CCO and a remarkably interesting reading also for all those who are interested in learning about the contemporary culture of doing business.

www.ingramcontent.com/pod-product-compliance
Lightning Source LLC
Chambersburg PA
CBHW031952190326
41519CB00007B/774